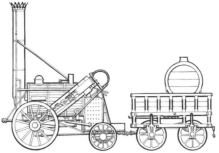

Introduction

This book is about a time of great change and revolution in British history. The Industrial Revolution resulted in the birth of the railways, huge steam powered factories and big cities, which were needed to house factory workers. The Agricultural Revolution brought farming in Britain into the modern age with improved methods of breeding, growing and new farm machinery. The French Revolution began a war which affected most of Europe and the American Revolution saw the birth of a new nation.

Some people rose and became heroes, men like Nelson, Wellington, Wolfe and Clive of India. Others like William Wilberforce, Robert Peel, James Cook and John Wesley made their mark in history with the legacy they left us. Mary Shelley wrote 'Frankenstein', J. M. W. Turner changed forever how artists painted and Dr Johnson produced a dictionary of the English language. Read more about these fascinating historical figures and learn about this exciting time in history.

Contents

Written & illustrated by William Webb
Front cover illustration by Les Ives
Published by Colour History Ltd © 2008
Print reference number 29658/04/08

The Georgian Kings

The Georgian kings suffered from poor reputations which forever coloured their reigns. The first two have been called stupid, the third lost America and went mad, the fourth was hated and the last, William IV, was nicknamed 'Silly Boy'.

George I (1714-1727)

Queen Anne of England had died without an heir as she had outlived all of her seventeen children. So the throne passed to the great-grandson of James I, George, the son of the Elector of Hanover in Germany. He arrived in England at the age of 55 and could not speak any English. He talked to his government in French, but spent much of his reign in Germany, relying on a cabinet of ministers to govern Britain. They were led by the First Lord of the Treasury, Robert Walpole, who is regarded as the first Prime Minister of Britain, although there was no such title at this time. This kind of government is known as a Constitutional Monarchy.

A Jacobite Rising

During his reign the Jacobites led a rebellion to put the Catholic son of James II, James Edward Stuart, the 'Old Pretender', on the throne, but the attempt was crushed. By law Catholics could not become king. Another disastrous event occurred which became known as the 'South Sea Bubble'. Many people bought shares in a trading business called the South Sea Company, paying ten times the true value of the shares. Eventually the company's promises were found to be lies and thousands of people lost their savings.

George I and his wife Sophia Dorothea of Celle in Germany

What a Way to Go!

George II died whilst sitting on the toilet. A post mortem revealed that his heart had exploded.

George II and his wife Queen Caroline

George II (1727-1760)

George I divorced his wife in 1694 after she ran off with her lover. The King had her imprisoned in a castle whilst her lover was mysteriously murdered. George II hated his father for the way he had treated his mother. Unlike his father, George II could speak English and was advised well by Walpole during the first fifteen years of his reign. The King trusted his wife, Queen Caroline, and the two enjoyed a very loving relationship even though he was unfaithful to her. He had been a soldier all of his life and was the last English monarch to fight on a battlefield. At the age of sixty he commanded the English and Hanoverian forces at the Battle of Dettingen in 1743, during the War of the Austrian Succession (1740-1748).

The British Empire Grows

In the latter part of his reign Britain fought in the Seven Years War (1756-1763). This was fought between Britain and France over land in America and later between European powers including Britain. The Prime Minister, William Pitt the Elder, advised the King about how to conduct the war. Near the end of George II's reign Robert Clive defeated the French in India and General Wolfe beat them at the Battle of Quebec in Canada. There was also one last attempt by the Jacobites to take the throne, but the revolt was brutally put down at Culloden (see page 6).

George III and Queen Charlotte

George IV and Queen Caroline of Brunswick

George III (1760-1820)

George II outlived his son Frederick, so when he died he was succeeded by his grandson George III. 'Farmer George' was very interested in the Agricultural Revolution in Britain (see page 13). He also took a keen interest in science. During his sixty year reign many great events occurred, such as the end of the Seven Years War, the loss of the American colonies, the French Revolution, the defeat of Napoleon, the invention of the steam engine and Captain Cook's voyages of discovery. You can read about these events in the pages ahead. George III bought Buckingham House, which is now Buckingham Palace, as a residence, but he preferred to live at Windsor or Kew. He was a popular king and the devoted father of fifteen children.

Prince Regent

During his reign the King suffered from bouts of madness which eventually resulted in his son, the Prince of Wales, ruling as Regent from 1811. Blind, deaf and mad, George III spent the end of his life at Windsor Castle. The Prince Regent earned a reputation for gambling, drinking, horse-racing and spending too much money on clothes and women. He had secretly been married to a Catholic widow, Mrs Fitzherbert, since 1785, but he officially married the wealthy German Princess Caroline in order to pay off his debts. When he first saw her he was so shocked that he nearly fainted. Her language and appearance were coarse and offensive in contrast to the refined tastes of the Prince. They married in 1795, but a few months after the birth of their first child they separated.

George IV (1820-1830)

In 1820 the Prince Regent became George IV. He was so hated that there were attempts on his life. When he drove through the streets, stones were thrown at his carriage and he had to be protected by soldiers. At his coronation the Queen unexpectedly arrived to reclaim her rights, but she was locked out of the ceremony at Westminster Abbey. She died shortly afterwards. The King spent most of the last part of his reign in bed at his magnificent pavilion in Brighton, or at Windsor Castle.

William IV (1830-1837)

George's child, Charlotte, died before him, so the throne passed to his 64 year old brother William. A keen sailor, he was unlike his brother with his unrefined manners and outspokenness. He had served in the navy since the age of thirteen and had impressed Horatio Nelson. He did not dabble in politics, but he did play a part in the passing of the Reform Bill of 1832, which gave more men the right to vote, particularly in the new towns and cities which had emerged during the Industrial Revolution. His reign saw the abolition of slavery in Britain (see page 16). On his death he was succeeded by his niece, Victoria.

William IV and his wife, Princess Adelaide

🐾 Did You Know?

The Prince of Wales's wife to be, Princess Caroline, rarely changed her linens and never washed, so she stank terribly and the Prince had to drink heavily in order to go through with the wedding ceremony. During their short time together they only communicated by writing to each other.

A Poem about the Georges

George the First was always reckoned
Vile, but viler George the Second.
And what mortal ever heard
A good word of George the Third
But when from earth the Fourth descended
God be praised the Georges ended.
Walter Savage Landor 1765-1864

An Age of Revolution

The British colonies in North America largely looked after themselves, but Britain controlled their overseas trade so that they could dictate the price of imported goods. When Britain captured French colonies in America an army was dispatched to prevent French reprisals.

The Boston Tea Party

The Americans were taxed to pay for the army, but the colonists demanded that they should not be taxed by a British parliament when they had no say in the government. The taxes were so unpopular that they were stopped, except for the tax on tea. Britain insisted that Americans could only buy tea imported by the East India Company and no other merchants. So, in 1773 colonists disguised as American Indians attacked British ships in Boston Harbour. They poured their cargoes of tea into the water, hence the name 'Boston Tea Party'. In retaliation Britain imposed strong penalties on the state of Massachusetts, but this only united the colonies in opposition and brought them closer to war.

The Shot Heard Round The World

A thousand British troops were ordered to march to Concord, Massachusetts to search for hidden arms. News of the 'redcoats' advance was brought to the colonists by a skilled silversmith and expert rider called Paul Revere, in his famous night ride. At Lexington about seventy local militia men dressed in ordinary clothes faced the British soldiers. Outnumbered, the American officer told his men to disperse, but when they hesitated the British surged forward. Suddenly a shot was fired and the war began. American poet Ralph Waldo Emerson later called it, 'the shot heard round the world'.

The American War of Independence

King George III regarded the Americans as rebellious children. He and his weak Prime Minister, Lord North, led the defence of British interests in America badly. In 1776 the American Colonies declared their independence, although about a third of the colonists remained loyal to Britain. The Americans were led well by George Washington and with French help they eventually defeated the British. The war ended in 1783 with the Treaty of Versailles. A victorious George Washington became the first President of the United States.

The War of 1812

During the Napoleonic Wars (see page 7) British ships stopped and searched American ships to look for British deserters and insisted that all neutral ships stop at British ports and pay a tax. Britain was also supplying an Indian chief named Tecumseh with weapons to lead attacks from the Canadian border. This angered the Americans who declared war on Britain. During the war the capital city, Washington DC, was burned by British soldiers. The blackened official home of the President was painted white to conceal the damage, which is why it is known as 'The White House' today.

Robert Clive

General James Wolfe

Other Conflicts

During the reign of George II the East India Company stationed soldiers in India to protect its interests. One of its clerks, Robert Clive, led a successful war to defeat the French and Indian armies. At the siege of Arcot in 1751, Clive and 500 men faced an Indian army of 10,000 men with elephants and artillery. After an hour the Indians fled from the battle. In Canada in 1759, a young General named James Wolfe captured the French city of Quebec by scaling its cliffs in a daring night assault. Within an hour the city had fallen, but Wolfe was killed in the fighting. These victories added India and Canada to the British Empire.

> ### 🐾 Did You Know?
> In 1777, William Pitt the Younger said in the House of Lords that, "If I were an American, as I am an Englishman, while a foreign troop was landed in my country, I never would lay down my arms. Never! Never! Never!"

The Battle of Culloden 1746

William, Duke of Cumberland, was the second son of George II. He was sent to Scotland to replace General Hawley who had been defeated by the Jacobite army at the battle of Falkirk. The 'Young Pretender' to the British crown, Prince Charles Edward Stuart, or 'Bonnie Prince Charlie' was now in control of the Scottish Highland Army. Despite the warnings of his clan chiefs, Charles's men stood all day without food ready for battle on a moor near Inverness, whilst the English army celebrated Cumberland's 25th birthday. The tired Scots launched a night attack which failed miserably as they lost their way in the boggy ground. The next day the English silently deployed for battle.

Cumberland's superior artillery bowled open lanes through the ranks of Highlanders whilst Charles dithered. The Jacobite right wing could stand it no longer and charged heroically into the smoke of English musket fire, to the shrieking cry of 'CLAYMORE!' They were cut to pieces, but still the brave Scots advanced and finally clashed with the English in bloody hand-to-hand combat. The English used a new tactic, bayonetting the opponent to their right where they had no shield for protection. It was all over within an hour. Charles fled from the battle and eventually escaped to France. 'Butcher' Cumberland's orders were to show no mercy to the wounded and fleeing Scots. This was the last pitched battle to be fought on British soil.

🐎 Did You Know?
The colonists formed themselves into armed militias and were known as 'Minute Men' because they were civilians who were ready to take up arms in a minute.

What do you think Britain and America would be like today if America had not rebelled against British rule? If America had remained part of the United Kingdom, how do you think this would have affected world events up to today?

The Napoleonic Wars

France was in a poor state after participating in the American War of Independence. There was not enough food to feed its huge population, few people had a say in how the country was run and unrest was fuelled by pamphlets calling for social and political reform.

The French Revolution

The French monarchy, the upper classes and the clergy lived in luxury and imposed heavy taxes on the people. Dissatisfaction finally exploded into revolution in 1789 when some Parisians stormed the Bastille, a prison in Paris. The French Revolution had begun and it was to throw all of Europe into war. In 1792 France became a Republic and a year later King Louis XVI and his Queen, Marie-Antoinette, were executed. Up to 40,000 people were guillotined during this 'reign of terror'.

Emperor Napoleon I of France

Many feared the revolution would spread to their countries. The execution of the French King and Queen led Britain and other European powers to form an alliance against France. The French army won many battles, thanks to a gifted general called Napoleon Bonaparte. In 1799 he made himself First Consul of France and in 1804 he became Emperor.

The Invasion of Britain

A brilliant naval commander destroyed Napoleon's fleet at the Battle of the Nile in 1798. Three years later the same commander defeated the Danish navy who were allied to the French, at the Battle of Copenhagen. Admiral Horatio Nelson had no sight in one eye and lost an arm in combat. In 1805 he was sent to destroy the French fleet near Cape Trafalgar in southern Spain. A French army of 150,000 men were ready to invade England in barges from Boulogne if the French were victorious against the English fleet. Twenty-six British warships sailing in two columns broke through the curved line of thirty-three French vessels. At the moment of victory, Nelson was mortally wounded, but the invasion was over and Napoleon did not try again.

Horatio Nelson (1758-1805)

Nelson's uncle was a captain in the navy. Nelson joined his ship at Chatham as a midshipman in 1771. He was small and quite weak and suffered from sea sickness. Despite this, within seven years he had made his way through the ranks to become commander of a small warship. He was promoted to Admiral in 1797. His bravery in battle, often leading his men in fierce hand-to-hand combat, earned the respect of his crew and fame back in Britain.

Nelson's Women

In 1787 Nelson married a widow named Frances Nisbet who had a five year old son called Josiah. Home life bored him and it was whilst he was at sea that he met the wife of the British ambassador at the port of Naples in Italy. Lady Emma Hamilton was very beautiful and after Nelson's victory at the Nile they became lovers. They had two daughters, one of whom survived infancy. After her husband's death in 1803 Emma lived with Nelson at Merton, Surrey. Although she inherited money from Nelson and her husband when they died, she squandered most of it and was later imprisoned for being in debt. She died a poor woman in France.

Horatio Nelson and Lady Hamilton

Yuck!

An 11 year old midshipman killed at Trafalgar described his diet. 'We live on beef which has been ten or eleven years in the cask and on biscuit which snakes your throat cold in eating it owing to the maggots, which are very cold when you eat them! Like calf's foot jelly or blancmange, being very fat indeed. We drink wine, which is exactly like bullock's blood and sawdust mixed together.'

The Battle of Trafalgar 1805

Nelson was an easy target wearing his full uniform with glittering medals and was shot by a marksmen perched in a mast-top on the French ship 'Redoubtable' as the battle raged on around him. One sailor wrote, '...all the men on our ships are such soft toads, they have done nothing but blast their eyes, and cry, ever since he was killed. God bless you! Chaps that fought like the devil, sit down and cry like a wench.'

HMS Victory

Nelson's flagship was constructed of 6,000 trees most of which were oak. She was very fast and could reach about ten knots, or 18.5 kilometres per hour. She was launched in 1765 with 104 guns on three gun decks and a crew of nearly 1,000 men. Their average age was 22 years old. You can now see this famous Georgian battleship at the **Historic Dockyard at Portsmouth.**

Life on Board the Victory

Seamen were often forced to join up. They had no uniform and did not receive pay until the end of a voyage, if at all, although they shared the booty from captured ships. They lived on the gundeck where they fought in battle and they slept in closely packed hammocks. They spent their free time playing games of dice and cards, telling tales, playing music, carving, drawing, practising knots or model making. Sometimes sailors sang sea shanties, or work songs, to help them do repetitive tasks such as hauling ropes. Women were not allowed on board, but unofficially some men had wives and officers sometimes brought their families with them.

There was no refrigeration or tinned food. Meat was packed in barrels with salt to preserve it. Cooking would help kill some of the taste of putrid meat. Fresh water stored in wooden barrels turned green and slimy, so ships put into port as often as possible to get fresh supplies. Seamen drank beer, wine or rum mixed with water, called 'grog'. Discipline was harsh and drunkenness was not allowed. Ten of Nelson's crew got thirty-six lashes each for drunkenness two days before Trafalgar. Disease was rife. During the war against France, thirteen times as many seamen died of disease and accidents than were killed in battle.

The Peninsular War

With the British gaining command of the seas, the conflict centred on the fight to stop Napoleon advancing across Europe. The scene was set for the rise of another great man, Arthur Wellesley, who became the Duke of Wellington.

The Peninsular War

By 1810, Napoleon's empire extended from Spain in the west to Russia in the east. The European powers formed an alliance to defeat him, but the battle on land was much longer. The part fought mainly by Britain was known as 'The Peninsular War' as much of it took place in the Iberian Peninsular containing Spain and Portugal. After years of fighting, Napoleon was defeated by the Duke of Wellington. The French Emperor was defeated by other countries too and in a disastrous war against Russia on his eastern front. Of the 115,000 men he took with him to Moscow only 10,000 survived. They had been ill-prepared for the Russian winter and many froze to death at night. Britain and her allies forced Napoleon to abdicate and in 1814 he was exiled to the island of Elba, between Corsica and Italy. However, Napoleon was not finished yet.

Soldiers Drink Blood!

To survive the freezing conditions on their retreat from the Russian capital city of Moscow, soldiers cut up the bodies of their starving horses. They used their skins for protection against the cold and drank their blood for nourishment.

🐎 Did You Know?

The Duke of Wellington had a very special address, it was Number 1, London. His home, Apsley House, is at Hyde Park Corner and can be visited today. It houses many beautiful treasures given to the Duke from grateful nations saved by his efforts. Other items he brought back from his campaigns include a colossal nude statue of Napoleon by Canova. In 1828-1830 he was Prime Minister of Britain and is remembered for his honesty and integrity as a politician, but his conservative views were not always popular. He died in 1852 in his official residence as Lord Warden of the Cinque Ports, at Walmer Castle in Kent.

There are six things wrong with the picture below. See if you can find them.

The Battle of Waterloo 1815

In less than a year after his exile on Elba, Napoleon returned to France and rallied an army. Britain, Russia, Prussia and Austria joined forces to oppose him. Napoleon's strategy was to divide the British and European forces under Wellington from the Prussian army under Prince Blücher, because if they combined they would outnumber him. However, he failed to win decisive battles against Wellington at Quatre Bras and the Prussians at Ligny in modern Belgium. Wellington set up camp on a ridge south of Waterloo village near Brussels. The night before the battle it rained heavily. Napoleon slept in a farmhouse, but boasted that the next night he would be dining in Brussels.

Napoleon delayed his first attack because he was waiting for the ground to harden so that he could move his artillery. He could not see all of Wellington's army because much of it was hidden behind the ridge. He began by launching a ferocious infantry and artillery attack on Hougoumont, a country house occupied by Wellington's forces, but amazingly it did not fall to the French. The main battle began with artillery bombardments, infantry advances and cavalry charging in support on both sides. One of Napoleon's generals made a huge blunder. On seeing the British fall back a few yards, Marshal Ney thought they were retreating and launched a major cavalry attack. Without infantry support, Ney's cavalry were mown down like 'grass before a mower's scythe', as the British artillery Captain described it. Despite the carnage, the French cavalry overran the guns and the artillery men escaped into the safety of the British infantry squares. These squares steadfastly held back wave after wave of cavalry and infantry attacks. The battle appeared to be at a standstill.

To break the stalemate, Napoleon committed his reserve infantry, including his loyal Imperial Guard. They advanced up a slope into artillery fire as if on parade, to the cry of 'Vive L'Empereur'. They were unaware of the British troops which had been ordered to lie down in the thick wheat on the other side of the ridge. Wellington ordered them to stand up and fire, which they did as one man. They obliterated the French. The arrival of Prussian reinforcements under Blücher sealed the allied victory. Napoleon was exiled to the island of St Helena in the South Atlantic, never to return.

Taking the King's Shilling

British soldiers earned a shilling a day, although expenses were deducted, but it was better than starving. Wounded men received a pension, as did those who stayed in the army for 21 years. A high ranking officer such as a colonel earned over 22 shillings a day. Officers came from the upper classes, which is why it was said that the Battle of Waterloo 'was won on the playing fields of Eton'.

The famous British infantry square was vulnerable to artillery, but presented a solid defence against cavalry and infantry attacks. A steady discipline, close-range musket volleys and the tight hedge of bayonets defeated the finest cavalry of the day. Known affectionately as the 'Brown Bess', the flintlock musket could fire up to five rounds a minute in the hands of a well-trained soldier. British infantry bayonets were nearly half a metre of sharp steel.

The Industrial Revolution

Advances in scientific knowledge in the 17th century laid the seeds for the industrial revolution which was to follow, with the start of scientific societies, mass production and precision engineering. Now centuries of traditional craftworking was to change very quickly.

Steam Power

In 1769 James Watt patented his improved version of the steam engine. Factories sprang up and many were powered by Watts' engines. In the last forty years of the 18th century, patents granted for inventions increased tenfold. Money was lent to entrepreneurs at low interest rates. The Agricultural Revolution and better living conditions meant there was a population explosion, which created a demand for new manufactured goods, as well as a plentiful supply of workers for the new factories.

The Spinning Jenny

The need for textiles made from cotton imported from America was satisfied by new mass production methods. In 1764 James Hargreaves built the 'spinning jenny' which enabled one worker to spin many cotton yarns at the same time. Craftworkers now became machine operators. You can see a jenny at the **Helmshore Textile Museum** in the Rossendale Valley, Lancashire.

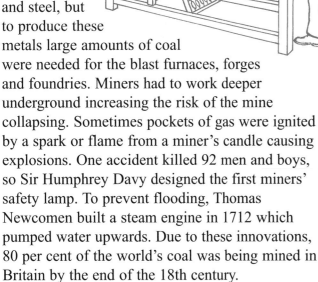

The Spinning Jenny

Mining

New machines and products were built of durable iron and steel, but to produce these metals large amounts of coal were needed for the blast furnaces, forges and foundries. Miners had to work deeper underground increasing the risk of the mine collapsing. Sometimes pockets of gas were ignited by a spark or flame from a miner's candle causing explosions. One accident killed 92 men and boys, so Sir Humphrey Davy designed the first miners' safety lamp. To prevent flooding, Thomas Newcomen built a steam engine in 1712 which pumped water upwards. Due to these innovations, 80 per cent of the world's coal was being mined in Britain by the end of the 18th century.

Canals, Roads and Bridges

Poor quality roads and primitive methods of transport created 'canal mania'. British engineers built a network of canals to transport goods and raw material in larger quantities at faster speeds. In some places people raced each other to buy shares in the new canals being built, hoping to turn over a quick profit. Around 1820, a Scotsman called John Macadam invented the tarmac road surface, which is still in use today. Another Scotsman, Thomas Telford, improved road building and completed the famous Menai Strait Bridge linking north Wales to the island of Anglesey.

The Menai Straits Bridge

Poor Conditions

Unfortunately the Industrial Revolution happened so quickly that regulations were slow to follow. Factory owners thought nothing about employing children as young as five, including girls, in dangerous conditions. Some suffered broken limbs or were severely burned by machinery. Workers were poorly paid and some worked up to eighteen hours a day, six days a week. Fearful of employees banding together, Parliament outlawed workers' societies and managers often exercised brutal discipline. A child who attempted to escape would be whipped.

Unrest Grows

In the north a group of craftworkers called 'Luddites' attacked and destroyed machines in several factories. In 1824 Parliament allowed workers to join a trade union, but in Tolpuddle in Dorset six labourers who formed a union were sentenced to seven years in Botany Bay in Australia. There was such an outcry that the 'Tolpuddle Martyrs' were pardoned and sent home. In 1833 the first of several Factory Acts was passed which improved working conditions for women and children.

The Age of Steam

In 1803 Richard Trevithick built a steam locomotive, but it was George Stephenson who pioneered rail travel in Britain. The Stockton and Darlington Railway opened in 1825 and five years later Stephenson's locomotive 'The Rocket' was used on the world's first public railway. It was the fastest locomotive of its time. You can see a replica of this famous steam engine at the National Railway Museum in York. The original Rocket is housed in the Science Museum in London.

George Stephenson
1781-1848

lowering bars

upper canal

barge

water-tight container is lowered to bottom

water-filled cistern

container　**barge**

lower canal

An ingenious canal lock near Bath enabled a barge to travel from a great height in seven minutes, instead of slowly going through a series of locks. It involved the barge and its crew being sealed in a watertight container and lowered inside a cistern. It was very dangerous and after some spectacular accidents the idea was eventually abandoned.

The Agricultural Revolution

Until about 1730 farming in Britain was not much different from the medieval period. Ploughs were often made from wood, fields lay fallow every three years and farm animals were slaughtered in the autumn due to the lack of food to feed them in the winter.

Enclosure

After 1730, following the lead of a few pioneers, landowners began to use scientific methods to farm their land. Many families were forced off their land by 'enclosure', a process by which landowners sought to make the land more productive. Although this meant hardship for many people, without the increase in food production there would have been starvation during the Napoleonic Wars.

The Industrial Revolution Benefits From Farming

Jethro Tull, a gentleman farmer from Berkshire, invented the seed drill which drilled holes in the soil and put a seed in the hole. Until then sowing seeds was done by hand not very efficiently. This increased bread production which in turn caused population growth and provided the workforce needed in the factories, without which the Industrial Revolution would have been slowed down.

Landowners Grow Wealthy

Viscount Townshend or 'Turnip' Townshend as he became known, discovered that certain crops either added or removed nutrients in the soil. Introducing turnips for instance, was beneficial to the soil and meant that fields did not have to be left fallow. It also meant that there was food for the livestock during winter. Sheep breeding was improved by Robert Bakewell and this enabled England to dominate the wool trade. Bakewell carefully selected animals to breed specifically to produce more meat. This further helped population growth as there was now more food available. Thomas Coke, the first Earl of Leicester, increased his income almost ten times on his estate at Holkham in Norfolk by further improving breeding methods. His slogan was, 'No fodder, no beasts; no beasts, no manure; no manure, no crop.'

Food Glorious Food!

The Georgian period gave some people the chance to become very wealthy through trading and business. People lived in the newly planned towns with squares, streets and crescents neatly laid out. They enjoyed the new theatres, restaurants, cricket, horse racing and especially gambling. Eating was an important pastime for the rich who ate huge amounts of food. A typical day might start with oysters and bread and butter for breakfast, followed by a midday snack. Dinner at around two o'clock could be a partridge, goose or swan, then cakes washed down with fine wine. Supper was like another dinner and might include fish or roasted lobster. Tea to drink was expensive, so smuggled tea and home-brewed beer were very popular.

Writers, businessmen, scientists and politicians frequented the fashionable coffee houses to exchange gossip and the latest ideas.

The Grand Tour

Wealthy young Englishmen regarded the 'Grand Tour' as an important part of their education. The English tourist spent one to five years travelling around the major towns and cities of Europe accompanied by a teacher. In Paris he might learn fencing and how to woo a lady. In Rome and Florence he would marvel at the beautiful art and architecture. In one peak year Europe was crowded with 40,000 Englishmen!

The Poor

The poor lived on bread with cheese or butter, some vegetables and occasionally the cheapest meat, which they put into a broth. Because of their hard life, many were often drunk from drinking a strong drink called gin. In the first half of the 18th century, gin consumption rose ten times. They enjoyed cock-fighting, bear and bull-baiting and prize-fighting.

Georgian Fashion

Poor people wore simple clothes which had been handed down or were homemade. The wealthy bought very elegant and richly ornamented clothes. Large 'perriwigs' gave way to smaller powdered wigs for men. The man (far right) is wearing a silk waistcoat and velvet jacket with a lace cravat. The lady wears a dress shaped over hoops.

During the 'Regency' period, named after the Prince Regent, a man named Beau Brummell influenced taste. People stopped wearing powdered wigs and washed their hair instead. As a result, men and women did not need to wear perfume to hide their odours. This man has a top hat and tight trousers called pantaloons and he wears a simple neck cloth.

Women's wear changed greatly, but by the end of the Georgian period it was very simple in style. This lady has a high-waisted dress and bonnet. Because of mechanisation, printed fabrics became cheaper to produce and could be worn by poorer women. Children now had their own styles and simpler clothes instead of wearing adult styles.

In the country, landowners competed with each other to build the finest homes in the 'Palladian' style (see page 17). Holkham Hall in Norfolk is a beautiful example. The architect William Kent not only designed the building, but he also furnished it. In towns people lived in simple elegant terraced houses like those at The Royal Crescent in Bath.

Living Hair

Many fashions came from France, including the high coiffure. Hair was combed over a horsehair pad attached with pins and decorated with ribbons, flowers or feathers. Some designs would include a basket of apples or flowers, or even a ship with rigging, guns and sails. Insects made homes in these elaborate designs and so a 'scratching stick' was essential.

Operagoers often showed off their amazing coiffures. Design your own fantastic hairstyle which can include anything you can imagine.

The poor lived in small 'back-to-back' houses which were one room deep with a small alleyway between the next row of houses. The whole street shared one water pump. Each house had an earth toilet. A family lived in one room about 3.5 metres square and slept in one bed. Another family would live in the cellar below. Factory chimneys polluted the air with their thick smoke. Families in desperate need of shelter and food had to go to a workhouse where they would be split up and had to sleep in dormitories. A typical job might be breaking stones to build new roads.

Government and Social Reform

Life for most people was very hard and even the death penalty, or the threat of being transported to plantations in America, was not enough to stop people from turning to a life of crime. Theft, piracy, smuggling and highway robbery were rife.

Diseases like tuberculosis and smallpox killed large numbers of people, especially infants. Deaths from drinking gin rose alarmingly in the first half of the eighteenth century. Rioting was commonplace. Gloucestershire had so many riots in 1734 that the army was called in to restore calm. The government struggled to deal with these problems and to preserve law and order.

Prisons Under Pressure

Prisons were overcrowded and with the loss of the American colonies there was nowhere to put the increasing prison population. Ex-navy ships with their masts removed were made into floating prisons on the River Thames and elsewhere, but a new solution to the problem had to be found.

Transportation

In 1787 the first fleet of British ships set sail for Botany Bay in Australia. The ships carried 759 convicts, 119 of which were women. Most were thieves, pickpockets, conmen, counterfeiters and prostitutes. The youngest was a thirteen year old boy. Some of the sailors took wives from the convicts and their children became the first European Australians. Many prisoners died in subsequent voyages to Australia, as the job of taking them was given to slave traders. The local Aborigines died from smallpox and other diseases caught from the new settlers. Prisoners had a few more privileges than those back home and could be given positions of responsibility. Once they had served their time many became wealthy merchants, magistrates, artisans or farmers.

> ### ✒ Did You Know?
> Lord Lovat was the last person to be beheaded in Britain in 1747. He was an eighty year old Jacobite supporter. There was such a large crowd watching the execution that the grandstand collapsed killing twenty-two people.

The Peterloo Massacre

In 1815 the price of corn was kept at a fixed level to protect the interests of English landowners and labourers' wages. Imports of cheaper foreign corn were limited by imposing import duties. In 1819 a crowd of about 80,000 people gathered in St Peter's Field in Manchester to protest about the Corn Laws. Soldiers were sent in with drawn swords to arrest the leaders of the demonstration. Eleven people died and 400 were badly wounded. As a result, the government banned demonstrations, but support for reforms grew.

Robert Peel (1788-1850)

In 1822 Robert Peel was made Home Secretary. He improved the crime laws and created the first police force in Britain for the city of London. Unlike the armed soldiers at the Peterloo Massacre, the Metropolitan Police were not armed. Despite his earlier opposition to lifting the ban on Catholics becoming MP's or holding public office, he helped to bring this about in 1829. He later became Prime Minister.

Reforms

Towards the end of the Georgian period, more people could vote and 'rotten boroughs' were disappearing. These were areas represented by Members of Parliament which had no voters or where the people had to vote for their MP or face eviction from their home. Christian men and women such as Richard Oastler and Elizabeth Fry worked hard to improve conditions for the poor. Oastler campaigned for shorter working hours and an end to child labour, whilst Fry improved the treatment of prisoners, hospital patients and the insane.

Revival of Religion

As people moved to newly created towns many stopped attending church. A clergyman named John Wesley preached to the working classes in the open air. This was unpopular with the Church of England, but eventually Wesley founded the Methodist Church. George Whitefield was another preacher who preached sermons in the open air and together they saw a revival of Christianity.

Slavery

The major European powers had bought slaves from African chiefs since the 15th century. By the end of the 19th century millions of men, women and children had been crammed into crowded ships to be auctioned as slaves in America or the West Indies. Those who survived the trip were treated cruelly on the cotton and sugar plantations. A slave's life expectancy was about six years. Slavery was very important to the European economy. Once emptied of slaves the ships returned laden with sugar, rum or cotton.

Thomas Clarkson together with a group of Christians called the 'Clapham Sect' and led by the MP William Wilberforce, campaigned to end the slave trade. Slave ships were banned in Britain in 1807, but slave traders continued their business until slavery was finally abolished in 1833. Traders were paid twenty million pounds in compensation. The Clapham Sect established a colony in Sierra Leone in Africa for freed slaves. The British government took over the settlement and missionaries educated the population. Many became successful traders, doctors and lawyers.

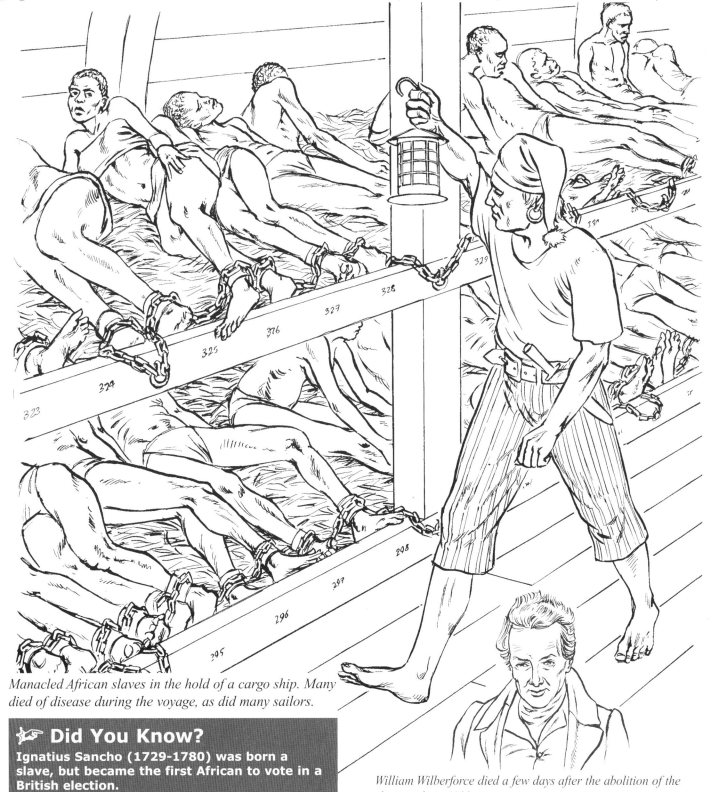

Manacled African slaves in the hold of a cargo ship. Many died of disease during the voyage, as did many sailors.

🐟 Did You Know?

Ignatius Sancho (1729-1780) was born a slave, but became the first African to vote in a British election.

William Wilberforce died a few days after the abolition of the slave trade in 1833.

The Arts

Missionaries had been reporting about the wonders of Chinese culture since the 17th century. The Georgian period felt the greatest impact of Chinese style, which influenced architecture, gardens, furniture, porcelain, the theatre and even philosophy.

Gentlemen studied the philosophy of Confucius, whilst ladies carried Chinese parasols. Homes were decorated with hand-painted Chinese wallpaper and Chinese-style furnishings made by Thomas Chippendale. The Scottish architect Sir William Chambers came back from China and published an influential book on its buildings. He built the pagoda at Kew Gardens in Surrey. Wealthy people redesigned their gardens in the Chinese style. They went to see operas and plays with Chinese themes.

Architecture

The 'Palladian' style was also popular and was based on Italian Renaissance architecture. Ancient Roman architecture was another influence on building style. Robert Adam and his four brothers were famous for their interior designs in these styles. A good example of Adam's work can be seen at **Stowe House** in Buckinghamshire. The original formal gardens at Stowe were replaced by 'Capability' Brown whose sweeping, natural designs became a model for English gardens.

Painting

John Constable painted some of Britain's most enduring images of country life, such as 'The Haywain'. J. M. W. Turner was the inspiration for future artists with his impressionistic landscape paintings. Thomas Gainsborough and Joshua Reynolds became renowned portrait painters of famous people and wealthy families. William Hogarth, Thomas Rowlandson and James Gillray drew inspiration from London life and made political humour and cartoons popular.

Literature

Dr Samuel Johnson was a famous writer who produced a 'Dictionary of the English Language' in 1755. His life and renowned wit were recorded by his friend James Boswell in his popular biography of Johnson. Daniel Defoe wrote 'Robinson Crusoe' based partly on a true story. 'Gulliver's Travels', published in 1726 was written by Jonathan Swift and was a criticism of how people lived. Jane Austen produced many of Britain's best-loved novels including 'Pride and Prejudice' and 'Sense and Sensibility'. Mary Shelley gave us 'Frankenstein' or, the Modern Prometheus'.

The Romantics

Poetry enjoyed a golden age with the 'Romantic' movement. William Wordsworth, Lord Byron, Percy Bysshe Shelley, Samuel Taylor Coleridge, William Blake and John Keats wrote poems which contained great emotion, in contrast to the cold, scientific ideas of the day. A farmer called Robert Burns became Scotland's national poet. His poems are celebrated on 'Burn's Night' every year.

Philosophy

The Scottish philosopher David Hume, inspired by the scientific advances of men like Isaac Newton, challenged Christian faith with the idea that knowledge must be based on human experience. He influenced another Scottish philosopher called Adam Smith. In 1776 Smith wrote 'The Wealth of Nations' which discussed the idea of how workers and employers could better society and their quality of life. His arguments promoting economic growth based on shared goals have influenced economists up to the present day.

Music

Music-making was a popular pastime and audiences could enjoy the new symphony orchestras in theatres and hired halls, which now blended individual instruments to produce a richer sound. They played music by composers such as Joseph Haydn and George Friedrich Händel.

The Royal Pavilion at Brighton

The Royal Pavilion at Brighton started life as a simple farmhouse. It was rented by the Prince Regent as he had been told that seawater would help his gout. He fell in love with the town and between 1815 and 1823 the famous architect John Nash turned the farmhouse into the spectacular palace we see today.

Nash superimposed a cast iron framework over the original building to create an Indian-style palace with domes and minarets. The interior is a mix of Chinese and English styles, filled with dragons, pagodas and mythical beasts. The Prince was famous for his parties, his extravagance and his mistresses. He married one of them, Maria Fitzherbert, in a secret ceremony and kept her at Brighton in high style (see page 4).

George Townshend (1724-1807) inherited **Tamworth Castle** in Staffordshire in 1754. He was a Field Marshal in the British army, an advisor to the King and a renowned caricaturist. During the war in Canada against the French, he was under the command of General Wolfe. The two men did not get on and the caricatures Townshend made of Wolfe tell us a lot about their relationship. George's son rebuilt large areas of the castle to reflect the popular gothic Georgian styles. The castle's Great Hall was used by the father of Robert Peel (see page 15), who was also called Robert. He was one of Britain's top industrialists and established cotton mills in the area. He employed 15,000 workers and used the hall as a blacksmiths' workshop.

Read a national or local newspaper and find a famous person, politician, or story you think would make a funny cartoon. Make sure you exaggerate the article, so that it is much funnier and then exaggerate the appearance of the people in your picture. Provide a caption which helps to explain what is happening.

Science

In the 18th century man discovered just how vast the universe is compared to the tiny world we live in. Astronomer William Herschel's telescopes found Uranus, the furthest planet known at that time and revealed that the Milky Way was not a cloud of gas, but a galaxy of stars.

James Cook (1728-1779)

James Cook changed the map of the world more than any other man in history. He was a brave and skilful navigator whose charts of the St Lawrence River helped General Wolfe land his troops and defeat the French at Quebec. After the war he was chosen to sail a small ship called the 'Endeavour' on a secret mission. He went to Tahiti with a group of astronomers who wanted to study the planet Venus, but his real orders were to find the southernmost continent. On his way back he charted the coast of New Zealand and part of Australia, landing at Botany Bay. On further expeditions he found Antarctica and many islands in the Pacific and Atlantic oceans. Sadly, he was killed by angry Hawaiian islanders. He was highly respected for treating his crew well.

The Chronometer

A prize of £20,000 was offered to the person who could create an accurate timepiece for a ship. With accurate timing a navigator could be very precise about his position at sea. In 1759 the clockmaker John Harrison created his 'chronometer', but unfortunately he was only given half the prize money. However, after a chronometer was successfully used by Cook on his voyages, George III personally intervened and a year before his death Harrison was awarded the rest of the prize money.

Harrison's chronometer

Vaccination

A risky way of making yourself immune from the deadly disease smallpox was to inject yourself with a small amount of pus from a smallpox victim. This was sometimes successful and sometimes fatal and you could still pass on the disease. The real breakthrough in fighting the virus came in 1796, when Edward Jenner carried out his famous experiment. He put pus extracted from the hand of a milkmaid who had cowpox into an incision on the arm of an eight year old boy. It was believed that milkmaids who suffered the mild disease of cowpox never contracted smallpox. Jenner demonstrated the importance of vaccination by proving that contracting cowpox provided protection against smallpox.

Woman Gives Birth to Rabbits!

With the explosion of ideas and scientific advances many crazy ideas were also seen. In London Dr. James Graham built a salon where childless people could recover their fertility by sitting on a magnetised bed. Mary Tofts had half of England, including George II's physician, believing that she could give birth to rabbits. She was finally caught bribing a servant to buy rabbits at a market.

This illustration is based on Hogarth's cartoon of Mary Tofts

> ### 🐾 Did You Know?
> From 1831 to 1836 Charles Darwin was a naturalist on board 'The Beagle'. The ship carried twenty-two chronometers. During the voyage The Beagle was one of three ships used to capture the Falkland Islands from Argentina.

Cook Lands at Botany Bay

James Cook lands at 'Botany Bay' which he named because of the 1,300 new flowers which were discovered on the east coast of Australia. The aborigines protested at his arrival with stones and spears, but the sound of musket fire, together with gifts of beads, ribbons and combs calmed them down.

The Bell Rock Lighthouse

Since the beginning of the 19th century the Bell Rock Lighthouse has proudly flashed its light to warn ships of the treacherous sandstone reef, which had claimed countless lives in previous centuries. Eleven miles off the east coast of Scotland, the thirty metre white stone tower dramatically rises out of the North Sea.

Designed by Robert Stephenson and another engineer, John Rennie, it is widely regarded as the finest lighthouse ever built. Its construction was a dangerous job which had to be attempted at low tide for two hours of each day in summer. It is made of dovetailed, one tonne blocks of stone, which did not need to be cemented together. The foreman, Francis Watt, devised special cranes to lift the blocks and temporary barracks were provided to house the builders in. After four years of back-breaking work, sometimes during violent storms and in ice-cold water, the 24 huge oil lanterns were lit for the first time in 1811.

GIANT GEORGIAN WORD SEARCH

H	G	P	A	U	R	A	W	R	A	L	U	S	N	I	N	E	P	N	R
I	E	R	C	A	S	S	A	M	O	O	L	R	E	T	E	P	A	E	E
N	O	I	H	O	R	A	T	I	O	N	E	L	S	O	N	I	T	H	I
O	R	N	B	G	U	O	L	R	A	V	I	D	A	B	G	R	T	T	L
I	G	C	T	E	U	M	I	O	R	E	E	T	O	R	A	E	N	A	R
L	E	E	E	C	T	A	S	N	N	Q	G	S	O	P	K	E	U	B	A
L	W	R	O	N	A	N	T	N	O	R	T	E	A	C	S	E	F	N	H
E	A	E	U	M	S	V	A	I	A	O	G	N	O	R	N	A	L	U	C
B	S	G	J	U	L	N	U	N	N	A	O	R	A	R	R	N	M	M	E
E	H	E	I	D	E	L	D	T	R	B	S	E	E	M	X	P	E	H	C
R	I	N	S	E	A	T	E	T	N	N	B	T	E	N	H	R	V	M	N
E	N	T	U	E	O	A	H	O	O	I	E	R	C	R	S	A	I	S	I
T	G	Q	E	U	P	U	E	S	R	M	G	U	E	M	O	S	S	V	R
I	T	R	R	A	R	L	N	T	O	E	E	Y	U	A	L	O	S	I	P
B	O	E	R	N	O	E	I	N	O	N	D	C	E	A	G	I	A	C	E
O	N	T	N	P	H	N	O	R	I	A	A	B	V	T	N	G	C	T	I
C	Y	I	A	P	E	R	G	I	V	A	E	E	E	A	A	E	G	O	N
A	S	N	E	C	H	E	E	Y	M	A	S	E	M	U	A	L	N	R	N
J	E	T	I	C	A	P	T	A	I	N	C	O	O	K	E	A	I	Y	O
C	S	L	C	O	O	L	R	E	T	A	W	F	O	E	L	T	T	A	B

Georgian	Farmer George	Bonnie Prince Charlie	Humphrey Davy
Napoleon Bonaparte	Captain Cook	Horatio Nelson	Stephensons Rocket
Peninsular War	Prince Regent	HMS Victory	Grand Tour
Queen Anne	Boston Tea Party	Slaves	Peterloo Massacre
Jacobite Rebellion	George Washington	Battle of Waterloo	Chronometer